The Danger of Ignoring Your Heart's Whispers

An Inspiring Journey of Self-Love and Empowerment

Natalie A. Southwell

ALL RIGHTS RESERVED. No part of this book or its associated ancillary materials may be reproduced or transmitted in any form or by any means, electronic or mechanical, including photocopying, recording, or by any information storage or retrieval system without permission of publisher. PUBLISHED BY: NATALIE A. SOUTHWELL ATLANTA, GA DISCLAIMER AND/OR LEGAL NOTICES While all attempts have been made to verify information provided in this book and its ancillary materials, neither the author nor publisher assumes responsibility for errors, inaccuracies, or omissions and is not responsible for any monetary loss in any matter. If advice concerning medical, spiritual, counseling, or related matters is needed, the services of a qualified professional should be sought. This book or its associated ancillary materials, including verbal and written training, is not intended for use as a source of medical, spiritual, counseling advice. The information contained in this book is strictly for educational purposes. Therefore, if you wish to apply ideas contained in this book, you are taking full responsibility for your actions. There is no guarantee or promise, expressed or implied, that you will achieve the results, strategies, concepts, techniques, exercises, and ideas in the book. Participants' results will vary depending on many factors. Check with your doctor, counselor, before acting on this or any information. By continuing with reading this book, you agree that NATALIE A. SOUTHWELL is not responsible for the success or failure of your personal or decisions relating to any information. PRINTED IN THE UNITED STATES OF AMERICA | FIRST EDITION © All Rights Reserved. Copyright 2023. NATALIE A. SOUTHWELL | Library of Congress Cataloging in Publication Data has been applied for.

To my guiding light, Jesus Christ, I humbly offer my gratitude for your unwavering love and for gently guiding me towards the path of liberation. In this newfound state of freedom, I am deeply thankful for the opportunity to be of service to others.

Dedication

This book is dedicated to two very special individuals - Jacque Mathews and Judy McLeod. These two amazing women have shared countless laughs and unforgettable moments with me. We were not just friends, but sisters, who shared the same faith, community of friends, and attended the same church.

Unfortunately, both Jacque and Judy departed their life before this book was published. However, I always carry their spirit with me, especially when taking care of myself. Thanks to their incredible guidance, I am blessed to be alive and well today. I would like to take a moment to honor and cherish the memory of these remarkable women who have left an indelible mark on my heart and soul.

Acknowledgments

First and foremost, without my tribe there would be no me, no book, and life would not be as fun and adventurous. So much of me would be unfinished and incomplete. You know who you are.

To my brilliant husband Crispin - You are my rock, my soulmate, and my constant foundation of strength. From the very beginning to now, your unwavering love and sacrifices for our growth and family never go unnoticed. Your support of my persistent changes and new endeavors has enabled me to flourish and catapult me into my destiny. I cannot thank you enough for allowing me to be true to myself and for standing by me through thick and thin. Your love and unwavering presence in my life have been a true blessing, and I am forever grateful to you. Thank you!

To my handsome sons, Shaquille and Shamari - You are the wind beneath my wings, lifting me up and inspiring me to be the best version of myself. Your gift of reason and honesty has been a source of accountability and growth for me, encouraging me to explore and find joy in what makes me truly happy. I cannot thank you enough for the power you bring to my life, and for the lessons you teach me every day. As your mother, I am in awe of the incredible young men you have become, and I am honored to be a part of your journey. I want you to know that I am endlessly proud of you both, and I am committed to supporting you as you continue to live in your truths and with limitless courage. You are my greatest blessings. Thank you!

To my mother, Martha and brother Darnell, my forever source of emotional provision - Your unwavering love and the bond we share as a family has yielded comfort and strength for me during the toughest days. Whether I need a sounding board to share my thoughts or a good laugh to lift my spirits, your presence and words always provide just what I need. I am grateful for the way you keep me grounded in the rich history of our family, reminding me of our roots and the love that always keeps us close. I cannot thank you enough for being a constant bridge of love, wisdom, and laughter in my life. Thank you!

To my prayer partner, Shelia, a true anchor and warrior in Christ - Your unwavering gift of friendship and accountability has been an incredible source of support and motivation for me on this journey. Without you, this book may still have been in the works, but you kept me focused on my calling and inspired me to stay on track. Your dedication and encouragement have been invaluable, and I cannot thank you enough for being a forever light in my life. From the bottom of my heart, thank you!

To Dr. Sonja Stribling, a powerhouse of kindness and passion. Your unwavering commitment to empowering and uplifting women who are called to speak authentically from their hearts is truly inspiring. Your encouragement and guidance have been invaluable to me, motivating me to step out of my fear and comfort zone into faith and action. Thanks for your mentorship and for being a trailblazing coach. I look forward to continuing this incredible journey with you, and I am honored to have you as a mentor. Thank you!

Contents

Dedication 5

Acknowledgments 6

Introduction: Awakening to Authenticity 11

Chapter 1: Finding My Truth Amidst Expectations 20

Chapter 2: Unraveling the Threads of My Past 38

Chapter 3: The Power of Awareness and Acceptance 54

Chapter 4: Rediscovering Self 67

Chapter 5: The Price of Silence and Submission 72

Chapter 6: Courageous Steps to Reclaim Life 75

Chapter 7: Nurturing Self-Love and Resilience 87

Chapter 8: Embracing the Journey to Wholeness 101

Chapter 9: Empowering Words for a Liberated Life .103

About the Author 105

Introduction: Awakening to Authenticity

Have you ever felt imprisoned by the expectations, opinions, and judgments of others? I've been there, feeling as if I were suffocating, lost, adrift, and unable to find my way. It seemed as if my world was collapsing around me, leaving me utterly alone with no one who could truly understand my plight. I, who once felt so capable, found myself spiraling downward, overwhelmed by work, stress, and the shackles of life, all while lacking the emotional resilience to cope. My world, as I knew it, seemed to be disappearing. As a woman of faith, I turned to God for guidance, and He showed me the way to break free from the chains that bound me. His divine intervention allowed me to escape life's pressures and burdens. Now, I am confident that my newfound freedom is not only for my own healing but also to help others in similar situations.

We, as human beings, are not machines. Our lives should be filled with grace, not consumed by anger, resentment, or rejection. If you're experiencing any of these negative emotions, it's crucial to trust in God to lead you towards salvation and deliverance. In my own journey, God revealed to me that fear was holding me back and that I needed to release it to truly flourish. It wasn't until I nearly lost my life that I understood the control fear had over me. God's grand plan for me was to let go of all forms of fear and fully trust in Him.

Did you know that fear comes in many shapes, not just the tangible fears of animals, attackers, or heights? Fear can manifest in more subtle ways, such as the fear of rejection, oppression, the unknown, uncertainty, or even the fear of saying no. The fear of saying no was one of the most debilitating and pervasive fears in my life. This fear robs you of your strength, character, and authenticity, infiltrating every aspect of your being. It's like a delusion in which you believe that saying yes will please others, even if it goes against your inner truth. By saying yes when you should say no, you've handed over your power. It's self-destructive to prioritize someone else's feelings over your own truth.

In doing so, you undervalue and harm yourself. You may not know how to say no tactfully or worry about hurting others' feelings. However, it's essential to understand that saying no is not inherently negative or stigmatized. In fact, saying no at the right time is an act of self-protection and self-defense, serving our best interests. It enables us to take control and steer our lives, rather than being a passive passenger on someone else's journey. It places us in the driver's seat of our own destiny. We must learn to establish boundaries and prioritize our needs. Saying no can be challenging, but it's a vital skill we must cultivate. When we say no, we take responsibility for our lives and set ourselves up for a more fulfilling and authentic existence.

There have been so many times when I said "yes" when I should have said "no." Time and time again, I regret not setting healthy boundaries for myself, feeling as if I let myself down. I made the mistake of prioritizing others' needs above my own, leaving me broken and shattered. This pattern continued for so long that I lost sight of my true self. The constant burden of subjugation took a toll on me emotionally, physically, and spiritually, causing me to drift further away from my authentic self.

I found myself being manipulated like a puppet, always fulfilling others' demands, even when it left me devastated, isolated, and full of regret. At times, I didn't even recognize myself, so consumed with pleasing others that prioritizing my own needs felt selfish. Looking back, I see how deceptive and disappointing I was to myself. Galatians 6:3 warns against self-deception, and I wish I had heeded its wisdom sooner: "If anyone thinks they are something when they are not, they deceive themselves." Proverbs 14:12 also reminds us that "There is a way that appears to be right, but in the end, it leads to death." Tragically, I was headed in that direction, with the end of the road fast approaching.

Deception can take many forms, even disguised as pleasantries or gifts. But when you say yes to something you don't want to do, your "gift of yes" is sent with insincerity, resentment, and dishonesty. In the long run, if left unaddressed, resentment can breed negative emotions and frustrations in relationships, leading to further conflict, especially if the other person fails to recognize your "gift of yes." It can be confusing because only you know the truth within. Continuing at this pace, you may feel taken advantage of, with your opinions or thoughts disregarded.

Putting others first felt sacrificial like I was doing it for them, being noble. They benefited from my generosity, but in hindsight, it was just virtue signaling to gain their approval. The more I did this, the more broken and sadder I felt. The weight of constantly saying yes became too much to bear on all levels. Those on the receiving end of my gifts had the mindset of "take and take" as long as I was so generous. Not all of it was their fault, but often it felt like exploitation at the expense of my goodwill. When this happened, I experienced emotional pain, abuse, and sometimes manipulation.

For years, as a people pleaser, I would always say yes to others' requests without considering my own needs. Agreeing to take someone to the store when I already had plans, sending an email for my boss when I was on sick leave, or accommodating my family, friends, or co-workers' schedule at my own expense, I had established a dangerous pattern of behavior. By always saying yes, I set a precedent that I was always available, regardless of the cost or how I was feeling. Over time, I realized this behavior was unsustainable and harmful to my own well-being. I needed to learn to prioritize my own needs and set boundaries for myself. I had to remind myself that my plans mattered too, and it was okay to say no to others in order to honor my commitments to myself. It's vital to recognize that your plans and goals are just as important as anyone else's. By championing your own commitments and sticking with them, you'll feel a sense of pride and accomplishment. It's okay to put yourself first sometimes and say no to others. It's not selfish; it's self-care. Ultimately, when you take care of yourself, you'll be better equipped to care for others.

My pastor often reminds me that when we tolerate fear, our faith becomes contaminated. Living in fear of people and their opinions is unhealthy and a sign of low self-esteem. When you operate from this place, you fail to champion yourself, your ideas, your likes, and your dislikes. This sets you up for failure, allowing others to win easily in some areas and causing you to relinquish your faith. Moreover, you surrender your power to the person you fear, allowing them to intensify that fear. You may struggle to accept that it's fear, but the reluctance to challenge the status quo or the avoidance in your heart proves that you are timidly renouncing your power.

Your power is your protection and armor. It defines who you are, and it's the first thing people notice when they encounter you. Being a kind-hearted woman is wonderful, but being a powerful woman is even better. It's as if you own your space, and the rewards are much greater. Living in fear is not a recipe for success. Fear, when channeled appropriately, can propel you towards safety, security, and the successful handling of threats. However, it shouldn't be something you constantly operate in. For this reason, strive to live fearlessly every day.

The essence of this book is to embolden you to take charge and hold yourself accountable for your own life. While it may not provide solutions to all your fears, it encourages you to face your past, reevaluate your beliefs, and address areas of fear and self-doubt. At its core, this book revolves around the concept of self-love and demonstrates how neglecting self-love or self-care can have disastrous consequences on your choices and, ultimately, your life. It offers practical approaches to help you evolve into the best version of yourself. Remember, your fears do not define you, and with faith and the guidance provided in this book, you can triumph over them. By taking proactive steps and embracing the love that elevates your spirit and nourishes your soul, you can rise above your fears.

Chapter 1: Finding My Truth Amidst Expectations

In my professional career, I became known as an "ambitious" leader and a "high performer." I enthusiastically took on substantial projects, collaborated with larger teams, and worked long hours to ensure the prompt execution and successful completion of challenging objectives. My leadership style was courageous, and people loved working alongside me. However, even with my high standards, I sometimes faced doubt and uncertainty, especially when I found myself in unfamiliar roles. I grappled with understanding domain knowledge, cultural subtleties, ways of working, and navigating complex organizational structures. I worked for major retailers with high demands, and I agreed to most things asked of me, which resulted in an unbalanced work-life.

Despite the pressure, I expertly managed multiple responsibilities and expectations, leading by example and motivating my team to excel. I held strong convictions about my tasks, projects, and deliverables, but also operated with adaptability and grace when collaborating with others.

In the corporate world, staying afloat often requires treading water. My survival strategy involved always having a "life jacket" in the form of backup plans, ensuring tasks were completed and project members felt empowered. Despite challenging and stressful times within the organization, I consistently delivered top-notch results that impressed colleagues from different business units. However, this pace of work was unsustainable, and it started to impact my health and family life. I lost sight of myself as I prioritized my career above all else, even at the cost of my well-being.

There were moments when I found myself saying "yes" when I really should have said "no," and dealing with the fallout was always challenging. I would leave situations disorganized or in turmoil, knowing deep down that I should have turned down the request. I felt this sense of duty to always say "yes," as if I couldn't say no to any request or task. But in time, I recognized that sacrificing my own well-being and happiness for the sake of my job just wasn't worth it. I discovered that establishing boundaries and having the courage to say "no" when necessary is vital for both my personal well-being and long-term productivity.

Sadly, I missed out on so many of my children's school events, games, concerts, and even their spring breaks. I would make excuses, telling them I had a demanding project that needed all of my focus. My husband and I were constantly on the go, chasing success, financial rewards, and recognition for our professional achievements. In the midst of our busy lives, we lost sight of the time we should have spent together as a family.

I would often ignore my inner voice urging me to say 'no' to certain tasks or commitments, thinking that I could handle it all. But each time I did, I neglected my own needs and struggled to manage my time effectively, which ultimately led to burnout. I remember holding my bladder during long meetings, not wanting to offend anyone or cut the meeting short. Unfortunately, this self-neglect turned into a habit and eventually led to health issues. During one of my annual reviews, my manager encouraged me to learn to say "no" without feeling guilty. Her words resonated with me, but as you can imagine, it's not easy to change a deeply ingrained trait rooted in past experiences. Although there were times when I felt guided by a higher power to decline a meeting, assignment, deadline, or work crisis, I would often ignore those promptings and take on the additional responsibilities.

Imagine landing a new job, one that pays more than you've ever made before. It's all too easy to fall into the mindset that we need to work even harder to prove ourselves, even if that means neglecting our loved ones, hobbies, and personal needs. Sometimes, others might even contribute to this burnout by imposing unrealistic expectations on us. While there are moments when going above and beyond is necessary, it's essential to recognize when excessive workloads are detrimental to our welfare. Neglecting our physical and emotional needs can significantly impact our health and overall quality of life. We must remember that taking care of ourselves isn't selfish; it's vital for our health. Our bodies are like sacred temples that need proper nourishment, rest, and care to function optimally. We have to listen to our bodies and give ourselves the time and attention needed to heal and rejuvenate.

Ignoring symptoms can disrupt our natural response mechanisms, and over time, they might become so muted that we no longer feel them, leaving us numb. I experienced this first-hand during a previous role. I became so numb to the pain I felt that it was physically draining. Despite my efforts to maintain a healthy lifestyle - eating well, walking, exercising, staying hydrated, and stretching - I found myself working non-stop under immense pressure for days, months, quarters, and even years until my body couldn't take it anymore. There were days when I could barely walk, as my back ached from hours of sitting in meetings. My knees swelled, and I developed circulatory issues in my legs. My daily step count plummeted from 10,000 steps in a day to just 10,000 a year. Sleepless nights and round-the-clock problem-solving blurred my days together, making it difficult to distinguish one day from the next.

My chiropractor and other specialists were astonished by the stress I was under and would check in on me periodically. My ability to retain information reached an all-time low. Struggling to focus, I worried I might be suffering from dementia. Brain scans from integrative clinics revealed that I was constantly on high alert, as if under attack. In contrast, during non-stressful moments, my brain scans showed a completely different picture. As much as I tried to manage the physical pain, I knew something had to give – but I just didn't know what.

During this period, my family life was suffering as well. My children and husband needed my attention, but I poured all my energy into my job. The pressure, the money, the demands, the heavy responsibilities, and the incentives consumed me because high performance was expected. But this came at a significant cost to my health and well-being.

Strangely enough, even though I felt trapped, I found myself advocating for others and standing up for them, even when no one did the same for me. I was sinking, feeling isolated and alone. I recall attending 98 meetings within a two-week timeframe, striving to stay organized and resist the prevailing culture. At first, I thrived in this environment, but eventually, it began to suffocate me and drain the life from my spirit. I was gasping for air. For months, I relied on my mother to bring me lunch and a bottle of water because I never took breaks for myself, used the restroom, or even went for a short walk.

Meanwhile, I observed others in similar positions managing to take meetings while walking, driving, or during appointments. I couldn't help but feel they were exploiting the company, while I believed I needed to be physically present in the office at all times. This type of thinking was off base and dangerous. I was sacrificing myself, falling on the sword for my job. My main concern was what others thought of me, rather than attending to my own body's needs. I believed that true leaders led from the front, never taking breaks, cutting corners, or stopping their relentless pursuit. I thought they should demonstrate to their followers how to persist, and I wanted to embody that kind of leadership. But soon, I realized I was losing myself in the process, and the pressure was mounting within me.

At the beginning of this job, I made a point to start each day with positive affirmations, motivational messages, and uplifting quotes. They helped me stay focused on my purpose and maintain a positive attitude in the face of challenges. I shared these practices with my team and former colleagues daily. However, as daily crises emerged, I found it increasingly difficult to continue these motivational activities. Before long, those little inspirational messages faded away. Balancing inspiration with problem management became a challenge, especially when faced with high turnover and mounting pressure from other departments. Despite my best efforts to shield my team and manage expectations, I was continually engulfed by the culture of this environment. I believed I could tackle the giants, but as a new manager in this area, despite my years of experience and accomplishments, I struggled to negotiate authentically and ask for what I needed. I bore the burden and tried to wear many hats while still learning about my new responsibilities.

Eventually, I found myself struggling to keep up with the same level of output and execution as my peers who didn't share the volume of responsibility or problem management I did. It was unsustainable and turned out to be the most demanding role I had ever taken on. Saying "yes" to this job offer nearly cost me my life. I found myself running from something and signed the first offer that was afforded to me. I was excited and celebrated the new role with my family. Looking back, I should have waited for a more suitable role but the fire in my current role was burning intensively so leaped without looking back. I jumped from the frying pan into an inferno. My learning curve was steep, and as a former Program Manager, Senior System Engineer Manager, and now Senior Software Engineer manager, I had bitten off more than I could chew. Accepting all these expectations marked the beginning of my downfall.

I didn't ask for help, but I desperately needed it. Fear of being perceived as a failure, along with my pride, stood in my way. I was so focused on maintaining an image of success that I let myself and, in some regards, my team down. As a result, I didn't reach my full potential as a leader in that role. I kept pushing myself, even when I should have taken a break or said no. I was too afraid to admit that I needed help or that I felt inadequate. I became hesitant to speak up in meetings or share my perspectives. I felt I lost my voice and my influence. It was my perception that flawed my vision. This wasn't always the case, but operating from a place of fear of disappointment transformed me and led me to do things I wouldn't normally do.

As the leader, when I saw my direct reports struggling, I felt like it was my duty to take on more work. Despite my own struggles, others saw me as an example of someone who was learning and growing in their role, someone who could take on new challenges and opportunities. My acting was convincing, and my smile suggested that I was handling crises with ease, but in reality, I wasn't. It reminds me of a high school track meet when I ran the quarter mile. I didn't finish the race and hid in a tunnel, hoping no one would see me. When the faster sprinters passed me, I was devastated. I walked to the coach's area, ashamed. I thought I was fast and prepared, but I was completely out of my league. I felt the same way in this job.

During my time in Information Technology (IT) leadership, I often found myself as the sole African American woman among ambitious, career-driven men. The pressure was immense, and I felt compelled to match their pace - working long hours, evenings, and weekends - despite also being a mother, wife, cook, and homemaker. Their situations were different from mine, as many of their wives were full-time homemakers, not burdened with juggling work both inside and outside the home. Working for and reporting directly to men was challenging sometimes, as they expected me to meet their expectations just as a man would, yet I was a woman with additional demands to balance. I strove to emulate their strength and mental toughness, but they had support from their wives in some cases who managed their domestic responsibilities.

In contrast, I shouldered both my job and household duties, and if I didn't cook, my family's meal would be less desirable. I even enlisted my mother to cook for us to alleviate some of the burden. There were days where I barely had a moment to catch my breath before the next meeting or request. I took on more than I could handle, resulting in a chaotic and disorganized life. While my male peers in leadership appeared to manage just fine, I struggled because I was overwhelmed. The job became unbearable, and I tried to escape the rollercoaster, but my work ethic and defensive reasoning kept me on it, even though it cost me everything. The job's expectations and commitments drained the life out of me, and it still wasn't enough.

Finding a balance between my personal and professional life proved to be a daunting task. I attribute this to my stubbornness and pride, as I was hesitant to ask for help and struggled to communicate my needs professionally. Navigating unfamiliar territory, I encountered workforce pitfalls I had no prior knowledge of, and my childhood pride led me to internalize the drama, making it difficult to seek help while trying to prove myself just as capable as anyone else. It was tough to admit my lack of specific skills, but I trusted in the Lord to guide and provide answers when I didn't know what to do. Sadly, I didn't have many female role models in a male-dominated environment to learn from, but I was grateful for the opportunities I received and worked diligently to be twice as good as the next man and execute just as effectively. Expectations were high and multiple millions of dollars would be a stake if an issue wasn't resolved quickly. Somedays I would say I was okay, even when the pressure was too intense to bear but self-sacrifice had its consequences.

Being a "yes woman" led me to constantly agree with others, disregarding my own needs. I craved a change in my daily routine, but my struggle to say no left me feeling confined, like a wounded animal unable to escape its cage. I longed to break free from the chains of always saying yes, yet I feared the potential consequences. The prospect of conflict, explanation, arguments, and even conversation filled me with dread. This apprehension partly arose from my reluctance to disrupt the harmony or upset others but going with the flow appeared to be the most comfortable option, even if it meant sacrificing my own desires.

Growing up, I was taught never to let anyone know if I was struggling or needed help. I concealed my wounds and put on a brave face, even when I was hurting. I often considered asking for help, but my instinct always prioritized others' needs over my own. While seeking mentorship was helpful, it never seemed to last. I lacked self-love and sacrificed everything I cherished to make others happy. This mindset caused me great anguish, and there was a time when I no longer recognized myself. I wore clothing and shoes that others had bought for me, regardless of whether they suited my style or size. My image was defined by someone else.

It can be quite challenging to keep up with all the aliases, especially when some of them don't suit your liking. I began to resent how I responded to certain people and started questioning my lack of assertiveness and failure to be bold, which I desperately desired. I would shrink back in meetings and cower in fear of my own voice at times. I was afraid to stand tall and exude the greatness that I knew was inside me all along.

When I couldn't handle the trauma, I put my trust in God to guide me. I clung to the scripture Philippians 4:13, "I can do all things through Christ who strengthens me." However, I believe that my adversary knew my weaknesses of being performance-driven and used those very traits to chain me. I felt literally chained to expectations, commitments, and deadlines. The same control I was trying to escape was the control I was under. I felt like a Black woman who was put in a broken position to sail, not to sink. But that's exactly what happened. I sank like the Titanic. I saw it coming and tried to isolate the turbulence and prevent its devastation, but the tumultuous waves continued to overwhelm me.

When I reached my breaking point, my marriage was strained, my relationships with family and friends were compromised, and my health was suffering. I felt like a fish out of water, slowly losing my identity, convictions, values, self-confidence, and self-worth. I was plagued with physical aches and pains, and my adrenal system was in overdrive, leaving me with no energy to sustain my well-being. I had temperature regulation issues, digestive problems, and debilitating migraines and headaches that urged me to stop and take care of myself. Despite the intensity of the pain, I pushed through, believing that saying no was not an option.

Chapter 2: Unraveling the Threads of My Past

Reflecting on my childhood, I recall growing up in a time of societal division. My hometown was separated into the east end and the west end, with distinct neighborhoods delineating the two. The west end was primarily Caucasian, while the east end was predominantly African American. As a child, I became aware of the complexities of racial dynamics in America and how this limited exposure would impact my ability to connect with those who came from different backgrounds.

My education took place in largely African American communities, from elementary school through high school until 11th grade. In this southern town, I had minimal interactions with children and teachers from diverse backgrounds, which inadvertently perpetuated segregation and an awareness of racial differences. My upbringing lacked diversity, and I was mostly familiar with African American culture. At times, we even seemed to use a distinct dialect, which my family understood but became a challenge when I later encountered more diverse communities.

In high school, our family moved to North Carolina, in an area with a more diverse population. I transitioned from a predominantly African American environment to one where Caucasian students were in the majority. This shift led to challenges in connecting with my new peers and caused a culture shock. It wasn't until I moved away from my hometown that I truly grasped the stark contrast in populations. The curriculum in my new school was significantly more challenging, and my grades reflected this change. I went from being a straight-A student to an average one in some classes.

This adjustment highlighted my struggle to navigate the new environment and adapt to a different lifestyle. The students I met, who came from different backgrounds, often exhibited confidence and assurance that I felt I lacked. Instead, I sometimes compromised my authentic self to conform to their expectations. Whenever I encountered someone from a different background, I perceived them as difficult to relate to and, at times, indifferent. They seemed free to be themselves, while I felt apprehensive about expressing my own identity. I tended to behave in certain ways seeking approval rather than acceptance. My differences didn't feel welcomed, so I conformed to their standards to fit in. This marked the beginning of me downplaying my true self to please others.

As an African American woman, I've seen countless women in my family endure physical abuse and trauma at the hands of men and demanding jobs, sometimes to the point of physical devastation. I witnessed a matriarch, who worked in a factory return home from work hunched over and in pain from the laborious tasks all day, only to continue doing the same for her family at home. She felt she couldn't say "no" to such an exhausting job or find another one, so this family member persevered and prayed for strength. She sacrificed her health for the sake of providing for her family, and at the end of her life, she was bedridden or confined to a wheelchair. The inability to say "no" cost her dearly, but during those times, African Americans didn't have the freedom to act in accordance with their hearts due to laws of oppression and segregation.

Another example that highlights the impact of systemic racism in my life is when I witnessed one of the most respectful males in our family being called "boy" at a local store. He was a guardian angel to me and represented such strength, dignity, and great mannerism as a male and leader in our family. Seeing his humiliation as a hardworking provider stripped of his dignity and reduced to such a derogatory term was heartbreaking. It was a clear display of bigotry and hatred from a society that viewed African

Americans as inferior. In such situations, the fear of retaliation or harm to one's family often compels people to comply with such treatment. Even when their hearts tell them to say no, they say yes to ensure the safety of their loved ones. Unfortunately, such compliance only reinforces the status quo and perpetuates the cycle of oppression. In the past, standing up against racism had severe consequences, including the risk of being killed, hung, or enslaved by accusers, which left many with no other choice but to submit to their oppressors.

Growing up in such an environment, I grappled with finding my strength as a woman. Witnessing family members' compliance in the face of such disrespect made me realize that there are times when it's necessary to override your instinct to say "no" or stand up for yourself. It shaped my approach to certain scenarios and encounters, and these patterns followed me into my adult life and career. While I felt profound anger and sadness for my patriarch, I also admired the strength he displayed by silently enduring the treatment he received when, in his heart, he longed to confront the self-gloating and disrespectful man. I remember the pride I felt for him, as he expressed his anger in the car, yet was devastated that he had to dim his light at the disrespect of another. Understandably, there are times when you must override your conscious decision to say "no, this is wrong" or "how dare you treat me in this manner," but I learned that there are also times when creating a safe space to honor your heart is crucial. In this case, my giant's compliance saved our lives and allowed us to see another day.

This way of living had become both a model and a symbol of survival for me, influencing my decision-making and shaping my thought process as a woman. It has also introduced pockets of fear and apprehension when it comes to pleasing others in order to sustain life or achieve success. Being the only daughter in my immediate family, my mother insisted that I travel everywhere with my two brothers, never venturing out alone. They served as my guardians, chaperones, and protectors, making decisions for me, and I often followed their lead. Growing up in a fear-based environment fostered codependency, as I only felt safe when accompanied by my brothers.

I heavily relied on my brothers as defenders and decision-makers, instead of taking ownership of my own needs and desires. Saying "no" in their absence was a challenge, leaving me feeling vulnerable and lacking courage during pivotal moments in my life. Even when I didn't want to, I often complied with their instructions, fearing disapproval or negative consequences. This dependence on others took precedence and shaped my future, limiting my ability to express myself fully.

Walking in their shadow, rather than leading from a place of complete confidence in myself and relying heavily on their decisions, solidified my fear-based mindset. When they were not around, I found myself easily pressured or persuaded by others, as I didn't know how to say "no." This behavior wasn't a problem for me until I became an adult, a mother, a wife, a co-worker, a community leader, a manager. As a child, I took pleasure in being obedient and didn't challenge my parents or teachers. Being seen as the nice one, moldable, bendable, flexible, and adaptable was a badge of honor for me. However, this tendency left me vulnerable and lacking courage during pivotal moments in my life. My reliance on others took more precedence than I realized, shaping my future and leaving me seeking affirmations, validations, and approvals before taking certain actions. I lacked emotional fortitude in some regards, making it difficult to express my needs and desires. Even when I didn't want to, I did what I was told for fear of disapproval or negative consequences. My response was always, "yes ma'am or yes sir."

I also grew up in an environment steeped in family addictions which can profoundly shape one's propensity for codependency. I recently discovered that this trait was at the core of my decision-making, leading me to seek validation before acting or making choices. I also found myself using people pleasing mechanisms as a way to cope with dysfunctional relationships. This way of thinking is a form of subservience, and although I didn't engage in substance abuse, I unwittingly brought these chains into my career, marriage, and adulthood.

I came to realize that I was living an addictive lifestyle, but instead of being addicted to substances, I was addicted to seeking people's approval and lacked confidence. Hailing from a background of domestic violence, I learned that emotional abuse is just as real and damaging as physical abuse. While I escaped physical abuse, I found myself ensnared in a cycle of emotional abuse. Recognizing these patterns is essential for breaking free and living a healthy, fulfilling life.

I once shared with a family member the notion that people will treat you the way you permit them to. If you allow them to take advantage of your time and disrupt your schedule, it becomes your responsibility when you fail to prioritize what truly matters to you. It broke my heart to realize that this lack of self-respect meant I couldn't expect others to value me. Many people don't recognize that they create their own image and hand over the power to control them to others. I recall telling my brother that a male classmate had physically assaulted me after school one day. His response was immediate and resolute: "I don't care who this guy is or how big he is; he violated my sister, and he will pay the price." And indeed, he paid the price. My brother confronted him and took action to show that no one was allowed to touch his little sister. The guy was left bloodied on the bus, humiliated and remorseful for his actions. Although my brother faced a week-long suspension from school, he stood his ground. The truth is, you determine who has power over you, and you possess the tools to handle individuals who may seem more imposing. By applying this same principle, you can stand tall in the face of fear or oppression.

In one of my college classes, my professor conducted an experiment on leadership and followership. When I played the role of follower during the experiment, I noticed my behavior was childish, submissive, and aimless. I constantly sought guidance on what to do next, lacked boldness, and felt like a robot devoid of self-worth. My actions during the experiment surprised me. At the time, I didn't understand the driving force behind this behavior. However, I later recognized it was rooted in my upbringing, where I was taught to comply and not challenge authority.

This mindset can obstruct one's ability to create, excel, and effect change. When blindly following, you may lose yourself in someone else's shadow. However, when I found myself in a leadership position, I began to operate in an entirely different manner. During the class experiment, my professor observed me taking on a commanding role rather than a submissive one. Reflecting on it now, I understand that I wasn't necessarily groomed for either role. Instead, I played the part based on what was popular or being emulated around me. Today, years later, I can assert with confidence that both leaders and followers should embody similar traits, with neither role feeling superior or inferior to the other. Both roles carry immense value, and it's crucial to acknowledge and appreciate the strengths each individual contributes. Ultimately, it's about collaborating toward a common goal rather than exerting dominance over one another.

Looking back on the past 30 years, I recognize that there were pivotal moments when God was trying to guide me, but my natural instincts overrode His message. As I reflect on those instances, I see that fear of disappointment or failure held me back. I let the expectations and opinions of others shape my actions and decisions. It took time for me to comprehend that true freedom comes from within, and I am the only one who can grant myself permission to chase my dreams and goals. While it's vital to surround ourselves with supportive and encouraging people, ultimately, we must be brave enough to make our own choices and take charge of our lives. In 1 Samuel 30:6, David didn't succumb to fear or disappointment when his home was invaded. Despite the challenge, he encouraged himself, leaned on the Lord for strength, and discovered hope and focus. We must learn to trust our instincts and believe that we can create the life we desire. It may not always be easy, but it's necessary for living a fulfilling and purposeful life. Trusting the Holy Spirit within us is key to achieving our goals.

Not being true to myself made me miss out on opportunities and experiences meant for me. It was only when I started embracing my authentic self that I broke free from the expectations and facades holding me back. I learned that I didn't need anyone's approval or validation to be who I am. Moreover, I found that being genuine attracted the right people and opportunities into my life.

It's never too late to start living authentically. It takes courage and vulnerability to let go of the masks and expectations that have restrained us, but the rewards are worth it. Each of us is unique and has something valuable to offer the world. By accepting our authentic selves, we can lead a more fulfilling and purposeful life. My childhood experiences and family dynamics may have contributed to my inclination to adopt a persona and pretend to be someone I'm not. I saw family members putting on a façade to shield themselves or others, which may have subconsciously influenced me to do the same. Furthermore, marrying into a family with greater expectations and pressure to conform might have reinforced this behavior. However, I now understand that feigning to be someone I'm not, ultimately weakens my character and lessens my self-worth. It's crucial for me to remain true to myself and not succumb to someone else's expectations or ideals.

Do you see this pattern of behavior in yourself? Are you consistently seeking approval and pretending to be someone you're not? Such behavior can hinder your success. Remember, if God approves of you, then you are already approved. Seeking validation from others might feel good temporarily, but it can also prevent you from realizing your full potential. Perhaps this pattern is why you haven't launched your own business yet. You could be overshadowed by other people's opinions, concerned about their thoughts and judgments. However, you're the one in control and can choose your path at any moment. Don't let the fear of others' opinions determine your destiny or success. Take charge of your life and embrace your authentic self.

When you say "yes" to appease someone else, you compromise the gifts and talents God has bestowed upon you. Have you thought about what you're doing with all the potential within you? Each day that passes can lead you further from your purpose. Have you considered the people you're meant to impact? Your message, audience, tribe, village, and witnesses are waiting for the answers you haven't yet uncovered due to fear, doubt, lack of knowledge, confidence, self-doubt, self-reluctance, and even self-sabotage. Are you waiting for the "perfect" moment to act on your dreams?

Being a "yes woman" caused me to conform to others' expectations, neglecting my own needs. I longed for a change in my daily routine, but my inability to say no left me feeling trapped, like a wounded animal in captivity. I desperately wanted to break free from the chains of always saying yes, but I feared the potential consequences. The conflict, the need to explain myself, the possibility of arguments, and even the dialogue itself all filled me with trepidation. Part of this fear stemmed from not wanting to upset others or rock the boat. However, going with the flow seemed to be the easiest option, despite my own desires.

Chapter 3: The Power of Awareness and Acceptance

For years, I had been stuck in a cycle of toxic behavior that left me feeling drained, overwhelmed, and hopeless. It was a dark place that I didn't know how to escape from, but I refused to give up. Eventually, I found a glimmer of hope in an unexpected place - a Facebook group that offered an eight-week course on personal growth and transformation. Little did I know that this course would be the catalyst for the transformation I desperately needed in my life.

The course required me to confront the painful truths about myself and my relationships, and it wasn't easy. But through this process of self-reflection, I discovered a path towards freedom and self-discovery. For the first time in years, I was able to set aside all expectations and focus solely on my emotional and physical well-being. I took a leave of absence from work and made a commitment to prioritize self-awareness, self-need, self-identity, and self-care.

With the help of a team of clinicians, I began the journey towards healing and self-discovery. I learned that my mental and physical health were inextricably linked, and that the weight of others' expectations was taking a toll on my body and mind. I had been oblivious to the damage that was being done, but with the help of my support team, I began to understand the deep emotional wounds that I had been carrying for years.

It wasn't an easy journey, and there were times when I felt like giving up. But with every step forward, I gained a deeper understanding of who I was and what I needed to do to create a life of joy and fulfillment. Today, I am grateful for the journey, for the lessons I learned, and for the person I have become as a result.

If you are healthy, this advice may not be helpful, but when you have been operating at 100% and pain interrupts your ability to function, it's time to pay attention. Many times, I desired to self-care, but I felt that I was too important to take the time I needed to manage myself and step away from the battlefield. I found inner strength to continue going, but it came at a cost. It's important to remember that God is always with us, even when we make bad decisions. He was walking with me as I let others steer me, but He would whisper every so often that I was going down the wrong path. It's not that I silenced His voice, but rather my job amplified its voice with all the demands of performance and work. I was a people-pleaser and enjoyed the awards, accolades, challenges, and the feeling of importance. I was afraid to disengage or get off the rollercoaster of trauma because I was considered a great crisis manager. I excelled at it, and people would ask me to manage complex projects and make decisions for the organization, regardless of how it affected everything I loved.

The analogy of the small foxes highlights the significance of seemingly minor issues or problems that, if left unaddressed, can lead to significant damage in a larger situation or problem. It is crucial to catch these small issues early on to prevent them from becoming larger problems that can spoil the final outcome. Unfortunately, in the past, I ignored these small foxes and pushed myself to the point of exhaustion, fatigue, and brokenness, all in the name of "getting it done."

It became clear to me that I needed to take care of myself not only physically but also emotionally and spiritually. Learning to say no when necessary and empowering others to be accountable for their own tasks was essential. When we say yes to everything, we often overlook our responsibility to ourselves and put ourselves under excessive pressure, leading to burnout. Therefore, recognizing our tendencies and limitations, prioritizing our well-being, and setting boundaries are crucial to living a balanced and fulfilling life. We cannot always please everyone, and that is perfectly okay.

Looking back, I realize that my current state of brokenness wasn't caused by a single instance of saying "yes," but rather, by multiple occasions where I agreed to things when I really wanted to say "no." I did this to please others, despite feeling miserable inside, and ignored the obvious fact that I didn't want to participate in certain activities or go to certain places. However, protecting your boundaries and asserting yourself isn't as difficult as it may seem. You already possess the tools to do so, and with the right intention and timing, these tools can work wonders for you. If you fail to assert yourself, you will eventually reach a point of breakdown and lose touch with your true self. This way of thinking can have a detrimental effect on all areas of your life, not just your career. It gives those around you control over your decisions and actions, turning you into a puppet that tolerates things you dislike. This can lead to silent suffering and abuse. There were times when I was not the best friend, daughter, or mother because I diminished myself for the sake of others' opinions. For instance, when deciding on a restaurant, I would say, "I'm fine with wherever you'd like to go." I avoided taking the lead, even though I wanted to, because I was afraid of being challenged or not being liked. I took the easy way out, even when it was tough, and this led to a sense of deception and trickery. It was similar to how I hid in the tunnel during that track meet, and I did the same thing at work and in my marriage. Saying "no" meant potentially challenging others or being misunderstood, and I couldn't bear that thought.

When reflecting on my career and life, I've come to realize that I've found myself in this situation more than once. Each time, I make a promise to myself not to let it happen again, but old habits have a way of creeping back in. If you're wondering how to put an end to this cycle and change the way you do business, especially when it comes to saying no, the key is to invest in yourself. It's important to invest in carving out a better future, one in which you are in control and don't allow external expectations to dictate your decisions. Of course, this is easier said than done. The comfort of familiar habits and expectations can lead to complacency and a lack of willingness to change. However, change is a constant, and ongoing self-evolvement is crucial to build the confidence to say no.

Fear can keep you in a place longer than your heart desires. It can hold you back from moving forward, even when you know it's time to go. Despite knowing when enough is enough, fear, combined with faith, can convince you to endure and press through. While this may be true in some cases, for someone who is bound by fear, it can give them permission to remain in a perpetual cycle of fear, which is unhealthy. Fear can hinder decision-making, narrow thinking, and limit creativity, making it difficult to leave a job or a relationship. Anxiety can harm your physical well-being, and depression can leave you stuck in a withdrawn, isolated space. Therefore, it's essential to recognize when fear is holding you back and take steps to address it so you can move forward in a healthy, productive way.

Unfortunately, if you've been a yes-person for years, undoing the damage caused by your habitual agreement will take time. However, there's no need to worry because change is possible, and that's why you're reading this book. You have a curiosity for deliverance, and you're seeking understanding of why you operate in a similar fashion. Perhaps you can identify with my journey, or you know someone who does. Whatever the case, you have the power to identify your flaws and bring clarity to your life. Take a moment to pause and allow patience to do its work. You owe it to yourself to be free.

I can recall how the expectations of the ministry became overwhelming, and I would drop everything to serve and support my pastors or the work of the ministry. I was even encouraged to give up my time for the work of the Lord. It felt satisfying to sacrifice, and I believed I would be rewarded for it. Perhaps it was because a laborer is worthy of her hire, and as you sow into the ministry, you will reap a harvest. However, I urge you to be cautious not to get caught up in the religion of sacrifice. Jesus is our ultimate sacrifice, and we don't necessarily need to sacrifice to receive God's love, support, or forgiveness. Let's focus on sharing love instead.

What if you were to pass away before your business or dream becomes a reality? If you are currently in a stalled position because you are waiting for permission from yourself or others, you are doing yourself a disservice and committing an injustice because your fear of taking ownership is greater than the opportunities available to you.

Don't get me wrong. Permission has its place when a child seeks validation or approval to take a specific action. However, as you become an adult, you must put away childish things, including the need for approval. 1 Corinthians 13:11 says, "When I was a child I spoke like a child, I thought like a child, I reasoned like a child. When I became a woman I put away childish ways." Instead of seeking affirmation for an idea, identify what's causing the need for permission. If seeking permission is doing more harm than good, then why not seek information on "how" to achieve your dream or business instead?

What fears are holding you back? Are you so consumed with seeking acceptance and worrying about what others think that you neglect your own desires and needs? If you don't pursue your dreams, who will? Think about how many people have left this earth without realizing the dreams within them. It's heartbreaking, and it's one of the reasons why I'm writing this book. It's time to break free from the same bondage that once held me back, and this book is here to help you do just that.

When you say "yes" just to please someone else, you are essentially compromising the gifts and talents that God has equipped you with. Have you ever considered what you are doing with all the potential inside of you? Every passing day, you could be moving further away from your destiny. Have you thought about the people you are meant to impact? Your message, audience, tribe, village, and witnesses? They are waiting for the answers that you haven't yet cultivated because of fear, doubt, lack of knowledge, lack of confidence, self-doubt, self-reluctance, and even self-sabotage. Are you waiting for the "perfect" moment to arrive before you start taking action towards your dreams?

What if you were to pass away before your business or dream becomes a reality? If you are currently in a stalled position because you are waiting for permission from yourself or others, you are doing yourself a disservice and committing an injustice because your fear of taking ownership is greater than the provision available to you.

Saying "yes" when you should say "no" can become a trap that leads to procrastination and delay. It's crucial to prioritize your own goals and aspirations rather than sacrificing them for others. While saying "no" may not always be a bad thing in a balanced environment, it can become problematic when a leader is willing to fail for the sake of others who don't appreciate or reciprocate the protection being offered. This can lead to a sense of failure and a desire for victory that exceeds that of those being helped.

Difficulties can arise when you try to be true to yourself after having encouraged bad behavior. Perhaps this behavior was influenced by what you witnessed as a child, where a family member pretended to be someone they weren't to spare your life or protect the family. This pretense followed you, and you didn't even realize it. You learned how to turn it on and off. To make matters worse, you find yourself in domineering or controlling relationships where expectations are placed on you for how you should dress, wear your hair, speak, and behave. You feel that your identity is being questioned, and that you are not perfect without pretense. However, this begins to put holes in your character, and out of respect, you try to bear the brunt of appeasement and playing nice or accommodating. It's time to say "no" to them and "yes" to yourself.

Chapter 4: Rediscovering Self

The Follower Syndrome can cause you to sacrifice your identity in the pursuit of following. It can manifest in different forms, whether it be a person, place, or thing that you put your trust or faith in. While following can be admirable to a certain extent, when fear of disappointment takes hold, following can morph into an idol or a tool for self-permission that defines you. As you continue down this path, you may realize that you no longer resemble the confident, strong person you once were. Despite this, you may still find a false sense of security and happiness in the journey. The problem is that you are now on someone else's path, not your own. You have become a captive or pawn to someone else, when in some cases, you should be their leader. Your inability to say "no" has suffocated your existence, leaving you out of place and out of position. Can you see the damage that the Follower Syndrome has caused in your life?

You have the power to turn your dreams into a reality because they are uniquely yours and belong to you alone. It's important to honor your destiny and pursue it with conviction. However, there is a caveat to this journey. After years of following others, it may take time to unpack the layers of clothing that don't truly fit you. These hand-me-downs, shoes, and outfits that were given to you without your input may not reflect your true style. It's easy to accept them without questioning, but deep down, you may not like the color, heel height, open toe, or slippery bottom. In order to step out of the shadows, it took me months of healing, detangling, and evaluating who I truly was. When I became a "yes woman," I lost sight of myself and no longer recognized my identity. I realized that I had to stop accepting certain things and that I no longer wanted to tolerate mistreatment from others. It was a difficult process, but I sought help and prayed about it. God knew my heart and led me to paths of emotional, physical, and spiritual healing.

Operating from a place of fear can have a severe impact on your confidence, which is the ability to convincingly believe in yourself without any doubt. Fear can prevent you from leaving situations where God is calling you to move on from. It's the fear of what others might say or think about you that can keep you hostage in situations that you should have left behind a long time ago. Fear says, don't leave that job because it pays too much. Fear says, don't leave that toxic relationship because that's where your bread and butter is. Fear says you don't have enough experience to start your business. Fear says, God didn't tell you leave so you stay. Remember, God doesn't need you to defend Him. He has been wrongly classified for thousands of years, and dimming your light to protect Him is not necessary. It might seem heroic, but what God truly wants for you is to be free. If that means leaving a job you once prayed for, trust the love He has for you to guide you to the next one. He will be with you every step of the way, and He will forgive you if you make a mistake.

You have a relationship with Him, and in relationships, there is always a giver and a receiver. You give your heart to Him, and He receives it, and in return, He gives you faith, and you turn over your fear.

There is also a creative power inside you waiting to be unleashed. When you operate from a place of fear, you begin to doubt your abilities and question whether you are capable of achieving your desired goals. Remember that you are capable, and that you have the potential to achieve great things. Trust in yourself and in God's plan for you, and let go of fear. With faith, anything is possible.

During a recent conversation, a loved one pointed out how effectively I managed my career and served as a leader in the community. It came as a surprise to me because I had been downplaying my abilities and lost sight of my own capabilities and inner strength. I embraced their assessment and saw it as a new beginning because operating from a place of fear or agreeing to things when we should say no can leave us vulnerable to manipulation by others, who may pressure us into compromising our values and beliefs. This can erode our sense of agency and resolve, making it easier for them to take control.

Chapter 5: The Price of Silence and Submission

Unmanaged fear can come at a high cost, often compromising our well-being and emotional stability. Long-term emotional stress and trauma can keep our adrenal system on high alert, negatively impacting both our physical and emotional health. When we experience fear, our body and mind can enter a state of heightened alertness and stress, which can lead to a decline in focus, motivation, and confidence over time. However, fear can also be a powerful emotion that motivates us to take action. By learning to manage and overcome our fears, we can take an important step towards reclaiming our power as women.

In the past, I embraced a philosophy of conflict avoidance and decision-making behind the scenes, believing it safeguarded my ability to choose. However, this approach can lead to avoidance and make it challenging to explain your actions and reasoning. It can also fuel doubt, making it easier to question your decisions if they don't succeed. Saying no and engaging in conflicts takes skill and requires transforming fear and apprehension into productive communication. I used to experience anxiety during conflicts and struggled to process frustration, feeling as if it was a rejection and a personal attack. However, healthy conflict can be beneficial, serving as a strategic mechanism to articulate your reasoning for certain actions.

I see you, and I admire your bravery and courage. The mere fact that you've picked up this book indicates that you've responded to the call to liberate yourself from the chains of fear and self-doubt that have hindered you from reaching your full potential. Deciding to break out of the cycle of self-sabotage for the sake of your personal growth is daring and courageous, and it's a crucial step towards regaining your power.

Chapter 6: Courageous Steps to Reclaim Life

Ownership and Accountability:

Recognizing the need for assistance and acknowledging that fear may be rooted in deeper issues such as fear of rejection, lack of self-esteem, or fear of accepting your authentic self is essential. Identifying the underlying cause of your fear and seeking help can provide insight into your story and help you address the issue at its source. Take a moment to process, jot down thoughts to identify your triggers of fear. Making excuses for others and concealing their mistakes only perpetuates this cycle of delay and avoidance. It's time to take responsibility and establish clear boundaries and expectations. Looking back, I realize that my successful peers understood the importance of holding themselves and others accountable. By shielding my employees from failure and covering up their mistakes, I was inadvertently hindering their growth and potential. It's time to abandon this flawed thinking and empower others to stand on their own. It's time to stop enabling and start embracing accountability.

Maintaining regular accountability to your new truths or versions of yourself is crucial to prevent slipping back into old habits. Without a sustainability program for achievement, it's easy to lose sight of your goals and revert to familiar patterns. While no one doubts your capabilities, we are creatures of habit, and without someone to hold us accountable, we may fall short. Self-management is critical, and a lack thereof may have led you to this point. Therefore, it's imperative to seek coaching, check-ins, mentorship, and advocacy to help monitor your progress. Mentorship doesn't end when you reach your new version of yourself. It's an ongoing investment and goal-focused program that you should continue to invest in. A reputable coach who understands successful living and operation can help with accountability. Look for someone who can guide you through decision-making, the process of limiting beliefs, patience, and sequential thinking.

Counseling:

Taking the step to seek counseling is a crucial part of the healing process. It's essential to find a certified counselor who specializes in the specific area of your challenges. You can start by looking for local psychologists, master trainers, consultants, or certified therapists near you. You can also conduct an internet search to find reputable counselors. Even if you don't find the right counselor immediately, the fact that you have decided to seek help is a significant step towards achieving freedom and victory in your life. Remember that while you cannot change your past, you can certainly change your future. Each day, choose to put yourself first and celebrate your decision to seek change. Operating out of the integrity of your heart, start by forgiving yourself and thanking God for equipping you with His Holy Spirit to bring deliverance. Remind yourself how much you love your future and how proud you are for choosing yourself.

Saying No with Confidence:

Hold your ground and prioritize upholding your values, work ethics, and holding others accountable. By doing so, you are likely to experience less stress and pressure, while feeling more confident in your decision-making. This transformation is not about becoming rigid or unapproachable, but rather about developing strong opinions and convictions regarding your choices. It is okay to compromise and work towards favorable outcomes, but until you become comfortable saying "no" through practice, old habits may resurface. Breaking habits can be challenging, but there are numerous resources available to help create new ones. The primary objective of this book is to guide you towards recognizing and becoming more familiar with yourself. You did not reach this point on your own, so it is important to have accountable partners and coaches to support you along the way and ensure that you remain true to yourself. Let your close friends or loved ones in on your self-awareness journey. If they are true friends, they will walk with you during this process and even champion you for your courage to break free.

Forgive Yourself:

Your past does not have to dictate your future. Rather, you can use your past experiences as a catalyst for positive change. By examining what led you down certain paths, you can understand your drivers and make different choices going forward. This self-reflection is an opportunity to gain clarity on what motivates you, how you respond to different situations, and what your deep pains are. It's important to ask yourself tough questions about your past experiences: Was the pain self-inflicted? Was it caused by someone else's control or addiction? Did I lack the strength to see the truth? Was I afraid of the truth? Did I let my senses or sensual stimulation cloud my judgment? Did I allow myself to be punished or give people the benefit of the doubt? Was I unknowingly a people pleaser or conflict-avoidant? By digging deep and examining your past drivers, you can begin to understand how to rewire yourself for a better future.

You may be wondering if it is possible to rewire yourself. The answer is yes - it is absolutely possible to rework, reapply, reinforce, and rediscover oneself. Life is full of opportunities for self-discovery and growth. Listening to your inner voice can guide you through unfamiliar territory and times of reflection. You owe it to yourself to improve, master your fears and anxieties, and avoid self-destruction. Your emotions and feelings about circumstances drive your decisions, and it's important to be aware of this and learn to respond in a healthy and productive way. By overcoming your fears, you can avoid being limited or inactive and instead draw from a well of strength and courage.

Detach From Your Past:

Gather your past failures, hurts, and disappointments and throw them into a garbage bag. Let's take them to the dump and unload the deep-seated patterns of thinking that have held you back. Take some time to engage in activities that bring you joy and make you feel good about yourself. Whether it's taking a relaxing bath, going for a walk, or reading a book, do something that relaxes you and brings you satisfaction. Celebrate your successes along the way and take note of your progress. It takes courage and strength to break free from patterns of fear and say no to things that don't serve you. So, recognize your efforts and give yourself credit for the strides you make.

Be Unavailable:

It's okay to set boundaries and not always be available to others, and in fact, it's healthy to do so. When you make yourself constantly available to your boss, coworkers, or loved ones, it creates a sense of dependency and expectation that you will always prioritize their needs over your own. This can result in last-minute requests that disrupt your own plans and make it difficult to manage your time effectively. It's important to maintain accountability for the tasks that are important to you and resist the urge to reschedule planned activities to accommodate someone else's needs. For example, if you had scheduled time for a virtual training class but your partner asks you to help them with something, it's okay to say no and prioritize your own self-care. It's essential to communicate your boundaries and let others know that your time and schedule are valuable and deserve respect.

Neglecting your needs can lead to poor health and unaccomplished goals. While it's good to give to others, it's crucial to also love yourself and set clear demarcations that prevents over access to you. You cannot properly love and help others if you are unable to love and help yourself first.

Being flexible is great, but when it becomes your norm and you start neglecting yourself for others, it's a recipe for disaster. Your self-care is just as important as your commitment to others. Take the gym, for instance. It's your time to stretch, exercise, and take care of yourself. But when that time is cut short or interrupted, you're sacrificing your health for someone else. And that's why you're not in good health today. It's tough to admit, but you've been neglecting yourself for others. Sure, it's better to give than to receive, but what about that scripture that says to love your neighbor as you love yourself? How can you truly love your neighbor if you can't even love yourself? It's like the instructions that flight attendants give during an emergency situation: apply the oxygen mask to yourself before helping someone else. It's crucial because helping yourself gives you the strength to help others. Saying no to others and saying yes to yourself is what this is all about. What I'm saying is not for those who are self-centered and always say yes to themselves. The content is intended for those who neglect themselves for the comfort and well-being of others. Remember, people will treat you the way you allow them to. Set your boundaries and stick to them. And don't forget to reward yourself for your progress and compliance with your new truths.

Chapter 7: Nurturing Self-Love and Resilience

Shine Your Light and Live it:

Your light is your own. You alone are responsible for achieving your destiny. Don't blame others or life's trials if you fail. You can't use the excuse that you were aiding others in reaching their destiny, while neglecting your own. Learn to find your own path, and treat yourself with the same care and love that you give to others. Take care of your inner and outer beauty, your health, your career, and the person you are. You were born for a reason, to live the life God intended for you. Discover the new person God has created within you. Love and live your life. Don't let the stresses of this world steer you off course. Stay true to yourself and take someone else with you. Brighten someone else's day by learning from your experiences. Ask yourself, "How can I make your day better?" Show up for yourself, and don't let fear stop you. Walk in the direction of your desires, and be true to yourself.

Allow the Holy Spirit to Lead You:

You have the right to choose. God gave you the freedom to choose between good and evil, yes and no, right or wrong. What makes it special is that, despite your ability to choose, He provides you with the right direction to take. Do you ever feel the nudge of the Holy Spirit prompting you to turn left or right? Do you find yourself considering which direction to take based on your past experiences or what feels right to you? The Holy Spirit offers a guaranteed path to success, and even if you make mistakes at times, remember that failure is nothing to fear. If you do fail, forgive yourself and keep trying. It's up to you to own your decision and allow it to manifest in your life. Even if you've been on the wrong path for years, God is gracious enough to give us second chances and place people on our path to help us find our way.

Fear can make it challenging to assert oneself and stand up for personal beliefs, particularly in situations that require strength and courage. For instance, asking for assistance when necessary can be difficult when one is afraid of being exposed as lacking knowledge or experience, particularly in the workplace. This fear can cause people to avoid confronting issues that they should address directly, potentially leading to missed opportunities and self-doubt. Instead of being afraid or avoiding such challenges, you can take control of the situation by facing your fears head-on. This requires confronting fear directly, challenging its hold on oneself, and developing effective strategies to overcome it. Some proven methods include setting standards that provide protection from fear's influence, learning from past experiences, and sharing knowledge and insights to help others overcome similar obstacles. By taking these steps, you can regain your power, confront fear, and move forward with confidence and courage.

Start Your Day with Mindfulness:

Start your day with mindfulness and consistently give yourself time to create and affirm your day without any distractions. Set aside at least 30 minutes to an hour to listen attentively to your inner voice. You owe it to yourself to center your thoughts before engaging with others. Take the time to reflect on what your spirit, subconscious, and soul are telling you. This practice can help you gain clarity, reduce stress, and set a positive tone for the day ahead.

Stretch, Breathe, and Exercise Daily:

Engaging in physical activity, such as stretching, deep breathing, and exercise, has numerous benefits for the body. It triggers the release of endorphins, which are natural mood-boosters. Mood is a critical factor that can either motivate or demotivate a person, and incorporating physical activity into your daily routine can help alleviate pressure points and reduce tension caused by life events. It can also alleviate anxiety and restlessness, especially on days when high productivity is required.

Journal To Reflect On Your Wins:

Journaling is an effective tool for dispensing emotions and monitoring personal growth. By capturing your thoughts and feelings on paper, you can obtain a greater sense of clarity and perspective. Recording the challenges you faced throughout the day and the steps you took to overcome them can serve as a motivational instrument, encouraging you to continue moving forward. While some days may be more difficult than others, prioritizing self-love and reflection can lead to meaningful progress over time. By using journaling as a means of externalizing your experiences and capturing your journey towards a new identity, you can take an active role in your own personal development.

Treat Your Self to a Spa:

Relaxation can be an effective remedy for both physical and emotional fatigue. When you find yourself constantly sacrificing for others and trying to please everyone, your soft tissue and muscles are likely to be affected. This can result in adhesions and trigger points that contribute to the pain you're feeling. If you can afford it, consider scheduling regular deep tissue or medical massages with certified massage therapists who specialize in pain reduction. This can be a great way to help alleviate some of your discomfort.

Plant a Garden:

Gardening is a therapeutic activity that provides various benefits. It promotes mindfulness and allows individuals to focus on nature, which can enhance their outlook and mental stability, leading to reduced stress and improved overall health. Observing how nature responds to your efforts of growth and harvesting can be deeply satisfying and rewarding. There's a certain sense of fulfillment that comes with gardening, and it can positively impact your well-being.

Get Regular Health Check Ups:

Taking responsibility for your health is crucial, and no one can advocate for it better than yourself. Getting regular health checks is extremely important, especially if you have neglected your health in the past. Although your healthcare insurance provider can refer you to in-network or out-of-network doctors, it's also essential to partner with integrative medical specialists who can offer alternative perspectives to traditional medicine from a holistic approach. Integrative specialists can help you make informed decisions about your health and wellness, and work with you to create a personalized plan that addresses your unique needs.

Protect Your Calendar:

It's important to remember that you may have a tendency to say "yes" and give up on your plans for the benefit of someone else. This could be for your friends, family, church, ministry, or even work. However, the more you change your calendar to accommodate someone else, the more likely you are to find yourself feeling buried, unappreciated, unfulfilled, and overworked. It's crucial to prioritize your own needs and goals in order to avoid feeling burnt out and unable to achieve what you want.

Give Yourself a New Look:

As you work to transform your inner being, it's important not to neglect your outward appearance. Choose clothing that reflects the essence of your newfound self. This may require purchasing a few items that truly resonate with your personality and style. Opt for colors and shades that accentuate your best qualities. Avoid seeking the approval of others, as ultimately, it's your taste and desires that matter most. Cultivate self-acceptance, and don't be too hard on yourself if you're unsure of what you like at first. Consider visiting a women's clothing store and consulting with a wardrobe stylist who can suggest pieces for you to try on and experiment with. Above all, have fun with the process and the new You!

Take a Dance Class:

Taking a dance class has beneficial effects on creativity and expression. Dancing releases feel-good vibes and when you feel good about yourself, you tend to demonstrate happiness, joy, and laughter which in turn releases tension and pent-up energy. You can do it alone or with a group. Just know that when negative energy is released, the body responds with empowerment and improves your mind and body connection which is the process of self-care.

Champion Yourself:

I want to encourage you to take control of your life and your well-being. It's perfectly okay to say "no" and you don't have to be under anyone's control. You deserve to be free and to feel proud of yourself for protecting your state of mind. Remember all the people you've helped and championed along the way, and let them see you walking in victory. This is your time, so go for it and don't look back. If you do look back, let it only be to reflect on how far you've come.

Chapter 8: Embracing the Journey to Wholeness

Lastly, this list is just the beginning, and it's not an exhaustive one. Once you find your rhythms and justifications for self-care, you can add to this list and become a woman who is comfortable in her own skin, loves herself, dominates in life, and is free.

I took my power back each opportunity I had and when I failed, I didn't beat myself up. You shouldn't beat yourself up either. It takes time to reprogram the software of your mind that has been replaying on repeat. The day I took that courageous leap from life threatening yeses to boundless freedom was the day my life changed forever. It was breathtaking and I didn't care what anyone thought. Although I was afraid, I jumped and, on the way, down, there were other women cheering for me and waiting for me ready to embrace and celebrate my decision to liberate myself. I will never forgot the emotions that erupted from me as I said Yes to me!! It felt good! God is no respect of persons and if He did it for me, He can do it for you.

You were not born to live in fear or any type of bondage. Jesus came to set the captives free! Free from fear, free from the torment of saying yes when your heart screams no! Today is your day to break free from the bondage! You are no longer a people pleaser. You will no longer follow in the shadows of others. It's time to say "no," be assertive, and be free!

Chapter 9: Empowering Words for a Liberated Life

Today, on this date, I am breaking free from the chains of fear that once kept me bound and prevented me from being my true and authentic self. I will no longer allow myself to be a puppet or a "yes" woman for someone else's benefit. I am aware of the power within me and I am confident in my ability to say "no." I am a fearless, courageous, and brave individual who refuses to be trapped in a never-ending cycle of self-doubt and limiting beliefs about myself or others.

From now on, I have my best interests in mind, and I operate from a place of integrity, inner beauty, truth, and peace. I show love and kindness to myself, and I listen to my body's expressions and groans. If something doesn't feel right, I stop and pay attention. I no longer ignore symptoms just to please others or avoid offending them. Instead, I seek help and hold myself accountable for my own freedom.

I advocate for myself, even if no one else does, and I continue to love others while never forgetting to love myself. I am finally free from the shackles that once held me back. Today marks a new beginning, and I am grateful for the strength and courage to break free and live my best life.

About the Author

Natalie Southwell is a Senior Manager of a Fortune 50 company with an Executive MBA and PMP certification in Project Management. She has dedicated over two decades of her life to big box retail and corporate environments, particularly in Information Technology. While her career has brought her success, it hasn't been an easy journey without sacrifice and pain. In her debut book, "The Dangers of Ignoring Your Heart's Whispers" Natalie bravely shares her personal story of recognizing the dangers of constantly saying yes as she climbed the corporate ladder.

She is now the owner of the Essence of a Woman, LLC, a transformational professional coaching, consulting, and speaking platform, using her own experiences to guide others toward a healthier and more fulfilling career.

Helping women tap into their highest potential and catapult them to propel to a quality of living that they dreamed about. By investing in the lives of women, she hopes to foster freedom and create a positive, lasting impact.

Aside from her professional achievements, Natalie is a loving wife of almost 30 years, a proud mother, and grandmother.

Made in the USA
Columbia, SC
30 June 2023

19787255R00059